PROPRIET.

PROPRIETARY

POEMS

RANDALL MANN

A Karen & Michael Braziller Book

PERSEA BOOKS / NEW YORK

Persea Books, Inc.
277 Broadway
New York, New York 10007

Library of Congress Cataloging-in-Publication Data
    Names: Mann, Randall, author.
Title: Proprietary : poems / Randall Mann.
Description: New York : Persea Books, 2017. | "A Karen & Michael Braziller book." |
    Includes bibliographical references.
Identifiers: LCCN 2016058559 | ISBN 9780892554812 (original trade pbk. : acid-free
    paper)
Classification: LCC PS3613.A55 A6 2017 | DDC 811/.6—dc23
LC record available at https://lccn.loc.gov/2016058559

Book design and composition by Rita Lascaro
Typeset in Walbaum
Manufactured in the United States of America.
Printed on acid-free paper.

for Miguel Murphy

CONTENTS

ACKNOWLEDGMENTS

Grateful acknowledgment is made to the editors of the following publications where these poems, often in slightly different form, first appeared:

32 Poems: "Summer"
The Adroit Journal: "Fashion" and "Fiscal"
The Arkansas International: "Complaint"
Boston Review: "I Resign"
The Cincinnati Review: "Clinical Hold" and "Young Republican"
Copper Nickel: "*Leo & Lance*" and "Secondment"
Court Green: "Flagging" and "That Dark Apartment"
jubilat: "Black Box," "Blue-Sky Thinking," "Horizon," "Perspective," and "Rockstar"
New World Writing: "Gainesville"
Poem-A-Day (Academy of American Poets): "Alphabet Street," "Proximity," and "Realtor"
Poetry: "Almost," "Dolores Park," "Florida," "Halston," "Nothing," "Order," "Proprietary," and "Tender"
Redivider: "Control"
The Rumpus: "Letters from Satilla"
THERMOS: "Epithalamium"

"Black Box" and "Summer" also appeared on *Verse Daily* on January 25, 2015, and January 18, 2016, respectively.

"Day into Night" (under the title "Uncle") appeared in *Hot Sonnets* (Entasis Press, 2011).

"Etiquette" (under the title "For Thom Gunn") appeared in the feature "Share the Love" on *Poets.org* on February 14, 2013.

"Politics" appeared in *Van Gogh's Ear, Volume 4* (French Connection Press, 2005).

"Translation" (under the title "Sonnet 124") appeared in *The Sonnets: Translating and Rewriting Shakespeare* (Telephone Books, 2012).

The poems "Nothing," "Order," and "Proprietary" were awarded the J. Howard and Barbara M.J. Wood Prize from *Poetry* in November 2013.

Many thanks to Michelle Boisseau, Geoffrey Brock, Alex George, George O. Kolombatovich, Jackie Mann, Ralph Mann, Sabina Piersol, D.A. Powell, Aaron Smith, and Eric Smith. And thank you to Gabriel Fried for his faith in my work.

PROPRIETARY

PROPRIETARY

In a precisely lighted room, the CFO speaks
of start-to-start dependencies.
Says let me loop back with you.

Says please cascade as appropriate.
It's that time of morning; we all can smell
the doughnut factory. If scent were white

noise, doughnuts would be that scent.
The factory won't sell at any price.
The building next to it burns the animals

we experiment on. I have worked
on a few preclinical reports in my time.
The rhesus monkeys become

so desperate that they attempt suicide,
over and over again. I am legally obligated
to spare you the particulars.

How could things be any different?
Here many choice molecules have been born.
Here. This pill will dissolve like sugar.

Your last five months will be good ones.

NOTHING

My mother is scared of the world.
She left my father after forty years.
She was like, Happy anniversary, goodbye;

I respect that.
The moon tonight is dazzling, is full
of itself if not quite full.

A man should not love the moon, said Miłosz.
Not exactly. He translated himself
as saying it. A man should not love translation;

there's so much I can't know. An hour ago,
marking time with someone I would like to like,
we passed some trees and there were crickets

(crickets!) chirping right off Divisadero.
I touched his hand, and for a cold moment
I was like a child again,

nothing more, nothing less.

BLACK BOX

I was someone's
honor student once,
a sticker, a star.
I aced Home Ec and Geometry;

I learned to stab a fork,
steer my mother's car.
Old enough to work,
I refreshed the salad bar

at Steak and Ale,
scarcity a line
I couldn't fail.
The summers between university,

I interned at AT&T,
in the minority
outreach they called *Inroads*.
My boss, Vicki, had two

roommates, whom she
called, simply, The Gays,
crashing on her floor.
That was before

I was gay, I won't try to say
with a straight face.
Like anyone really cares
I care. What I'm trying to say:

all this prepared
me for these squat blinking
office accessories.
The dry drinking

after the accidental reply-all.
By now there's a lot to lose.
Little by little, I have become
so careful, no talk

of politics or orientation:
I let them say, he's a *homosexual*,
without an arch correction.
At a fondue buffet

in Zurich, our dumb-
founded senior group
director–when I let slip,
damn it, my trip

with a twenty-year-old–inquired,
They're always over seventeen,
right? I told her of course,
God yes, and, seething, smiled,

which I'm famous for.
I didn't want to scare
her. But I tell you,
I'm keeping score.

E-mail is no more
than a suicide
I'd like to please recall.
Note my suicide.

I'm paid to multitask,
scramble the life
out of fun:
Monday I will ask you–

every dash a loaded gun,
every comma, a knife–
to bury the black-box file.

ORDER

For once, he was just my father.
We drove to the Computing Center
in a Monte Carlo Landau
not technically ours. Lexington,

1977. That fall. The color
had settled, too, undone
orange-brown and dull yellow,
crimson. And it was something,

yet not, the pile of leaves
just a pile of leaves. Sorry to think
what thinking has done to landscape:
he loved punched cards,

program decks and subroutines,
assembly languages
and keypunch machines.
Even my father looked small

next to a mainframe.
The sound of order;
the space between us.
We almost laughed, but not for years—

we almost laughed. But not. For years,
the space between us,
the sound of order
next to a mainframe.

Even my father looked small.
And keypunch machines,
assembly languages,
program decks and subroutines.

He loved punched cards,
what thinking has done to landscape—
just a pile of leaves. Sorry to think,
yet not, the pile of leaves

crimson. And it was. Something
orange-brown and dull yellow
had settled, too, undone
1977, that fall, the color

not technically ours, Lexington
in a Monte Carlo Landau.
We drove to the Computing Center.
For once he was just, my father.

Horizon

Joyless,
devotedly boyless.
Everything,

the way
nothing is.
The point is this:

make
me less
than the lake

in the sheets.
The horizon
just above sex:

my thoughts
and prayers–
spots

and short hairs.
My itch;
my side-stitch.

Every day
can't
be lament.

An excuse
to lose
my shirt

for charity.
I feel,
if not real,

neon-real.
Sterile as hurt,
or parity.

FLORIDA

Like eelgrass through a glass-
bottom boat on the Silver River,
I see the state, obscured yet pure. Derision,

a tattooed flame crackling
underneath the lewd, uncool
khaki of an amused park worker.

I was the sometimes boy on a leash,
my sliver of assent in 1984–
as if it were my decision.

The I-75 signage, more than metaphor.
As if I had the right to vote.
The slumber parties then were hidden wood;

the tea so sweet, the saccharin
pink and artificial, like intelligence.
The science sponsored in part by chance.

I made my acting debut with the red
dilettante down the street, "Rusty" Counts,
in *Rusty Counts Presents: Suburbs of the Dead,*

straight to VHS. My parents phoned a counselor.
A palmetto bug read *Megatrends* on the fold-
ing chair by our above-ground swimming pool . . .

The pool shark lurked, but not to fear.
The end unknowable, blue, inmost, and cold,
like the consolation of a diplomatic war.

TENDER

There was a time
we had functional alignment.
I was your individual
contributor, you my associate

director. On Monday
I said *Happy Monday,*
rolling my rimshot grin.
Ring-fenced

by cool molecules,
like cattle, I battled biosimilars,
sipped local gin;
I tried my luck at affairs

and trade fairs,
optimistic as a fantasy
suite. I inked the deal,
the ink slick

and permanent,
like President
Reagan. I didn't sleep
unless I felt sick.

Something was always gated
on a fragile something.
Everything
on the critical path.

The whiteboard, cruel
as conceptual math,
scope creep
like a disease.

Some of those days,
our parent showed up,
bespoke shoes bearing Leckerli.
I felt like a starlet

on a cruisy backlot,
an outpost of opportunity.
I took on a new role,
went through the motions

and the typing pool.
But the bonus was no bonus,
any more than the bay.
Like tender, it started to fray.

My admin booked a good
weekend of atrocity. I winced.
I slid the To-Hurt folder below
a molecule's package insert.

Then came the Efficiency
Report, my resignation.
I packed up the brood
for Orlando, a last resort.

I cut off my khaki pants
at the knee, traded in the wife–
this is the Epcot Center of my life!
I want to thank you in advance.

I'd fallen out of favor, like a nation.

PROXIMITY

Out of the fog comes a little white bus.
It ferries us south to the technical mouth
of the bay. This is biopharma, Double Helix Way.

In the gleaming canteen, mugs have been
dutifully stacked for our dismantling,
a form of punishment.

Executives take the same elevator as I.
This one's chatty, that one's gravely engrossed
in his cloud. Proximity measures shame.

I manage in an office, but an office
that faces a hallway, not the bay. One day
I hope to see the bay that way. It all began

in the open, a cubicle—there's movement.
My door is always open, even when I shut it.
I sit seven boxes below the CEO

on the org chart. It's an art, the *value-add*,
the compound noun. *Calendar* is a verb.
To your point, the kindest prepositional phrase.

Leafy trees grow a short walk from Building 5.
Take a walk. It might be nice to lie and watch the smoky
marrow rise and fall, and rise. Don't shut your eyes.

REALTOR

Please
consider Ocean Beach
out of reach.
Try not to gulp
the green water
we porpoise
like employees.
My purpose:
your thought-partner.

There is a feeling
just shy of feeling,
like tongue on teeth.
Disbelief
hangs there,
an ill-chosen comma,
a lanyard with a pass.
I swear the train is coming.
I'm only here to help.

A client bought,
on second thought,
that *House in Vermont.*
Night is flirty words
with fiends,
the phlebotomists
from Quest
boning up on Thoreau.
It's too soon to throw

in the cards.
Live and let give?
Here. Let me give
you the *high-five.*
I searched;
my activism,
lightly starched.
I never meant
to live in euphemism.

Blue-Sky Thinking

This town is full of suits,
none of them in suits.
I can smell my VP,
dryer sheets and Listerine:

his streak isn't mean,
just mercilessly clean.
This town is full of flutes
aspiring to be filled.

It's March, 2013.
It's getting high, the S&P
(which I watch obsessively).
The yacht-rock trails off...

I hear you, he coos.
I get your fear.
It's almost curled.
It's almost third world,

the occasional cough.
The fear like cashmere,
casual as sweater
weather and beige.

And at our age!
Soy candles
and man-handles;
Pottery-Barn

party-bottoms.
The old thinking:
the sky, the color
of a wine cooler,

everyone says is blue.

Rockstar

Deadbolt the door on the way
out, and don't steal anything,
I say. I'm late. It'll take control
not to scream at that queen

who always takes two
seats on the train
when one will do.
The Rockstar, too,

free but undrinkable
at the canteen. I drink it all,
compare myself favorably
to Wallace

Stevens, but *seriously*–
I'm at a loss.
I repeat myself; I repeat
the same feeble

longing before town-hall
debates and first dates . . .
It's hard to say what I do:
I help the Statistics group say

what it never knew
it wanted to say–and fine,
what's most important
is passion, doesn't

matter what, cats online, poetry
(ugh); I find mine
are about landscape; Anne
Carson–do you know (never mind)

in her *Paris Review*, no me neither–
talked about background; oh,
well I am a mutt, Filipino, my mother,
Mexican-Puerto Rican-yellow–

don't know how I got this job either,
I have an MFA; sure, Jenny Holzer
used three of mine–
no, her admin, we're hella

tight or not; my first was with Jeff
Tweedy, he went into rehab, he left
right after via Chicago;
ha I am weird

about bowties, so wired,
too many polka dots, no
one else dresses up in San Francisco:
I am acting like a man,

these time zones, meetings, I mean
I love tricks who are sleaz-
y enough to bare me please–

CLINICAL HOLD

I am a silo,
breaking down.
I adjust my hair
in an Aeron chair;

the Swiss watch
while I take
a bio-break.
This campus-

cum-office-
park paints dotted-
line reports
for sport. Before

it gets old,
there's a re-org.
I know a cloud
(read: Legal)

keeps a log
of every load,
but shoot.
I order hookers,

my telecommute.
When FDA
weighs in,
it rings a bell...

Like hell,
the Clinical Hold
will be contested.
Three more years,

our options will be vested.

Secondment

In Basel, gnats appeared in the corners
of my room in the Messeplatz, no wish. I fished
hair and my own gloop from the shower–
lingering–spent evenings fingering

remotes in hopes of BBC 1 through 4, soft-core
cooking shows. I know. Forty's a bit late
for the grand tour. I caught a lot of the Eurovision.
At week two, an NYU student flew in, a little shy

of 21. I thought you said you were,
I thought. (My regret like a coat of spit.)
I thought about getting an animal. About golf.
I worked behind a big oak desk, someone's third-

hand idea of clout. The things I heard.
Freedom was a breezy lie, as was loneliness.
On the sly, I logged on to Planet
Romeo, for flesh: a torso wrote, *I want to dress*

you up like Norway, and invade. Let's forget it.
I went to Istanbul to see Mr. NYU, there
on a summer grant. I did it, but I can't.
In Kuzguncuk, a matted cat crawled out of filth

just to nuzzle me, my face. And I let it.

HALSTON

Roy Halston Frowick, 1932–1990

He kept his middle name, the pick of the lot,
he thought, and mispronounced himself: *Hall-stun.*

At Bergdorf's he acquired an accent and referred
to himself in the third person, every bird he flayed

wrapped in Ultrasuede. He lit a True with a True,
smeared his hirsute muse with sequins. There were air-

kisses, Capote's new-cut face at Studio 54, that Baccarat
flute of ejaculate. Never too late, he ordered in

meat and potatoes, and a trick.
He called it "dial-a-steak, dial-a-dick." He appeared

on *The Love Boat*, Halstonettes in tow,
maybe the high, maybe the low, watermark.

When his pupils betrayed him at work, on came the shades.
And a well-cut blazer, paranoia. He had signed away

the rights to his name, for options. When he tried
to reclaim them from the conglomerate,

he excused himself to the toilet, just a sec–
white dust on a black turtleneck.

His block started to look a lot like sickness.
Even his beloved orchids, the sickness.

Just like that, the eighties were gone.
New York, New York, the eighties were no one.

LEO & LANCE

for David Trinidad

I was seventeen
in Orlando,
heading toward

Orange Blossom Trail,
where the porn was.
Fairvilla Video,

its fried, freshened air.
I was terrified
but also thrilled,

on the edge.
Can anyone even
remember how hard-

won a little corner
of sex was then,
no internet,

no hope,
no combination?
I can't; I can.

In an
elaborate bid
to convince

myself and the clerk
I was bisexual,
I bought a bisexual

video
that I can't recall,
and a box

that made my heart stop:
Leo & Lance.
(VHS wasn't cheap:

I spent all
my allowance.)
I can measure

this adventure
in increments
of shame:

tape loop,
checkout,
the run-walk

to my red Buick
(no one could miss me),
the peel out.

And the drive home,
anticipation,
cruel cellophane...

Leo Ford,
born Leo John Hilgeford,
looked like California

by way of Dayton.
There was his tender
love of Divine,

that rumored three-way
on Fire Island
with Calvin Klein.

Late in his career
he raised rare birds,
volunteered

at Project Angel Food.
He was versatile:
so much to give.

And Lance,
David Alan Reis,
from Santa Barbara,

or maybe Oklahoma.
Poor orphan,
the stints

in jail,
IV drugs,
and conversion.

Leo and Lance
had the chance
to work together

twice on film–
Leo & Lance and
Blonds Do It Best–

and more than once
on the corner.
(Where have all

the hustlers gone,
anyway?)
They died

weeks apart,
in 1991.
Lance first,

in May,
in San Jose,
of AIDS complications.

On the death certificate,
his job is listed
as "model of clothing."

That July,
Leo on his motorcycle
was struck by a truck

on Sunset. "Chillingly,
Leo had played
a motorcycle accident

victim in *Games*,"
says IMDB,
so those who knew

his oeuvre
might have seen it coming.
After the wake at Josie's,

his ashes were scattered
by the Golden Gate Bridge.
A tree in India–

IMDB again,
as if the truth matters–
was planted in his name...

As I try
to get this right,
I pull up my cache

of scanned porn.
Leo & Lance:
it begins in synth,

Cali melancholy
canyon light,
and here's Leo,

shirtless,
running up a hill
in tight denim,

letterman jacket
thrown over his shoulder–
now the tinkling

piano; now's a good time
to jerk off
by the last of the snow.

God, bottle-blond Leo.
But wait, who
is that loping up the hill,

gawky, rugged, also blond,
a dumbfounded *wow*
uttered as he watches

Leo shoot? Of course:
it's Lance. Before
they formally meet,

before they go
back to the lodge
and do what they do

better than life,
they have a little snowball fight,
brief, unexpectedly sweet–

like children in the street.

Control

after Thom Gunn

I've been watching the debut film
by a splashy fashion designer.
The man loses his lover;
the woman drinks and, dismally,
cannot turn him straight.
Their lives click shut,
like a cigarette case.
An owl flies away, which must
foreshadow something.
It's really pretty tragedy.

I walk to the museum in the park,
to empty my head.
There's a lot of blown glass
by the man with an eye patch,
precious. Last
summer, in Venice,
I saw the most perfect thing,
a girl in a glass shop;
she worked there.
Her eyes were blue;
I wish I knew
how to describe them.
She was from Murano.
Made so exquisite
by her seeming lack
of self-knowledge.

But then I watched her
carefully
push her long hair over an ear,
and suppress a smile
in her hand mirror.
I was startled
by her control.

Break

At the Grab & Go
I learned
to skirt scandal.
It's only work-

place violence
if I leave my mark.
I took a pill; I lied.
Randall, don't.

Do not bribe her,
the hot intern,
a doughnut
dusted with ricin.

Trashy afternoons
in Borgo Grappa:
I miss eucalyptus,
vampires, buffaloes.

And the trek
back to Rome,
all that ration-
alist architecture.

Break,
let me make
up with you.
Let's cruise

the Ponte Milvio,
wrap a chain
around a lamppost,
lock it, and toss

the key into the Tiber.

FASHION

It was the age of paper. You slipped
me in your wallet, a crease of attention,
a string of numbers. *Sex is mathematics,*

or so said your favorite slasher novel,
but you weren't either one,
you were product placement,

a business-class-lounge
lizard, little hors d'oeuvre, ambition
a red ribbon curled on your chest.

You drunkenly rated your hotel rooms
by the strength of the jets in the hot tub.
Or the absence of said tub.

(One felt for the concierge.)
I need to hit the 9/11 for snacks, you joshed
on the phone, meaning 7-Eleven, meaning

an escort must have been on his way.
We laughed together but I knew
at that point you were too soon.

Between benders, you were Captain Rehab,
riding a wave of white chips. You held
your fancy water against the entire party.

Don't get it twisted, you told me, with a snap,
leaving *it* undefined. Your grand carelessness
seducing one or two of the uninitiated.

Back in the cul-de-sac,
you swung me in the crook
of your arm like a Birkin bag–

and you insisted on the Birkin.
You were the overheard whimper (you loved it),
the reluctant capitulation (loved it),

your industry a form of resentment (loved).
You were fashion–not fashionable, *fashion.*
Your jeans double-cuffed: you practiced.

You should have kept your flowered ties
and ACT UP tees from the nineties,
you lamented, they're *so fashion.*

You never followed through on *Silence=Death:*
The Musical, which is almost too bad,
really. Your inflection, another story.

You had exquisite taste, for a time,
but one differentiates the real from paste.
Your idea of slumming it was eating pho

in the inner Richmond, every noodle.
You were a circular
of circular facts

you were gobsmacked
(your word) I didn't know.
You squeezed the life out of everything

you had been given, or not given,
like a cock ring.

Perspective

Associations
are seductive and global.

Such gestures
seem almost primal,

though it's nothing of the sort.
One can waste

an hour one-upping
anonymous

in a text,
the right equivocation

and torso pic.
I lost 2010

trying to rhyme *sext*
with *sucked*, or *sacked*,

or, that's it, *sect*:
it's San Francisco,

for the love of Pete.
The meat

lolls on its silver plate.
On Market Street,

a pool of vomit,
a pigeon's meal.

I would eat,
but who eats.

My friend on meth
strapped his infant

to her car seat
one night all night

in the Tenderloin. All
we want

to feel is a full
roll of quarters,

not to feel.
We are art-house stars

in every back-room
and alley and stairs...

I have options:
undercut what I say

as soon as I say it,
or look you dead

in the face,
a parody of sincerity.

In the front room,
you should be fixing us

a drink, innocuous,
or spreading paste–

perspective–
while in the bedroom, listen,

things only a come-down twink
might dare condone

are proposed to my outcall.
I do. I believe we're done.

That Dark Apartment

When I returned from Kansas City, there were signs:
the spent hallway bulb, stack of *Chronicles*.
The dirt in wait for dirt. Heartless, the clichés;

artless, I mean. "Party guy seeks party guys,"
my meth-loving ex had typed on sites
with names like Adam4Adam and Manhunt.

"VERY open-minded," which was unlike
him, those caps. One last thing.
On Wednesday, midday, it was freezing,

but not for him; he came out of the den–
shirtless, hot, and blotchy–
when I summoned him. His pupils blown in the light.

"I don't do ultimatums," he said, let the door ease
shut, and turned up the porn. And burned up the lease.

Etiquette

We had no latex love to give
in blighted, half-remembered scenes:
to hollow boys in acid jeans
who asked to lose their will to live.

GAINESVILLE

When it started, I had been in Gainesville for three days.

They called him the Gainesville Ripper, which sounds comical, all but the ripping.

His name was Danny Harold Rolling.

It was August 1990.

Five of them were slaughtered.

I spent evenings huddled in the dorm rooms of my girlfriends.

There were lots of p-words tossed around, don't be a pussy, say a prayer.

When he was convicted, they sent him to Starke.

What a name for a town.

One drove slowly through Starke, a notoriously student-unfriendly place.

Whites were all right to stop there.

Rolling had lobster tail before the injection, an excellent if slightly clichéd choice.

Red Lobster on Newberry Road was relatively fine dining.

I spent much of the nineties in Gainesville.

Got two degrees and STDs in Gainesville.

"The nineties sucked," Marisa Tomei and Mickey Rourke declared in that ragged film *The Wrestler*.

No shit.

The nineties sucked, for me, in Gainesville.

There was the gay bar, the University Club, where I wore my J.Crew shirt, the Evil Flannel, where I danced and swallowed whatever the fuck.

We dropped Blue Monkey and stood on the balcony in the rainstorm.

I was the shirtless teeth-grinder in the corner with the lizard.

I was the tweaky late-night stroll by the green power plant.

I was the kid in the stacks of Smathers Library falling hopelessly in love with the poems of Donald Justice.

I fell in love, or what felt like love.

With gin.

With Salems.

With a boy.

We moved downtown.

We moved into a two-part apartment complex, one blue, one pink.

We had a wedding, in 1993, and my parents came, and they
stopped at Publix on the way and got a couple party platters.

The wedding was in our pink apartment.

Michael Hofmann, who lived in the blue, described it as "live-oaks
and love-seats, handymen and squirrels, / an electric grille and
a siege mentality."

An alligator crawled out of Lake Alice and ate a little dog on a
leash, said the *Gainesville Sun.*

I walked on Payne's Prairie with Debora Greger, in winter, and
imagined King Payne, the nineteenth-century Seminole Chief,
on a white horse.

The egrets were white. The heron was blue.

I narrowly escaped the controlled burn.

FLAGGING

And then I end up south of Market,
in the hands of a loaded man.
A few queens lean on the bar, in a file
and in leather,
the requisite drag.
It feels like I'm in a foreign land:

the walls by Tom of Finland.
The couples on the market.
My friend is becoming a drag,
so I scan the room for a suitable man.
(Damn I wish I'd worn some leather.)
With emery boards at the bar, I file

my nails; a Daddy asks me to defile
him. Why not. I paw his prostate gland
in the can: it, too, is leather.
The entire place is down-market–
and so am I. I love it. Man to man,
the ones in leather-drag

rarely call their leather "drag"–
it doesn't fit the profile.
A real man
should be able to land
a punch and leave a bruise, a mark, et
cetera, beneath all that leather.

Tucked into Daddy's leather
pants-pocket, a red rag:
there is always a market
for flagging, always the pocket-file
of symbol and
appetite. And I am the man

slipping into the back, like a woman.
The sunken faces taste like leather.
The back-room, like a gangland.
I fake a fight but let them drag
me to the corner. They're single-file:
each takes a turn, as one does, south of Market.

COMPLAINT

It was a lower-
    Nob-Hill affair, no shower,
no grower, our arc
    like an involuntary spit
at the urinal: a pull; a splash of blue.

How could one predict
    cozy slurs over sidecars,
strenuous humming?
    Parliament of scowls at the Owl Bar?
But what I would have given. To be a lone,

rolled, superfluous
    r in his world! Compliant,
I measure attempts
    at love against some fictive monster
alive. I lick a fleck of sleep from his eye . . .

The moon is a stye.
    The foyer, my brightest star.
Help me down the line
    of antibacterial goodbye.
The little black car on the screen is coming.

CALIFORNIA

Back in the Hale-
Bopp days,

there were precepts:
fair trade and beignets,

backup biceps.
How we could derail

a noun like brunch.
I always almost ate;

I was bloated
as a diva,

my saliva
Godiva,

my semen clotted
cream.

I wore a uniform,
tried to make the team.

I was this hood
as long as I could.

I feel like a urinal cake.
I drink from a urinal-ache,

unfrozen in December.
Humankind is a kind

of showrooming of the mind.
My self-abuse, going blind.

California
has metastasized.

STANDARDS

December. I fought
the urge to play "River," holed
up with my new Johnny.
I lived at the top of the hill,
he the bottom. Some joke. Joni
Mitchell was hot in that hiss-
ing bikini in 1975–remember?
As if the word hot
does her justice. I was three
in 1975, and Johnny...well,
waiting a while to be born.

This city is money to burn,
a cupful of change.
A burial urn
and a needle exchange.
The men like luck
to pluck
from a tophat,
wherever your tophat
might fall. The wall
of fame at 18th and Castro
is a slapdash memorial.
The faces change,
but this
will always be this.

The jaundiced
alcoholic with the Casio
plays standards
in front of the postcards
of the newly dead.
It's not a good time
for analysis.
Time is just a decent line:
the 24-Divisadero, or–
the 33-Stanyan!
The steady climb;
the convoluted turn.
Forever lovers hover;
a certain sour
smell of piss.

Dolores Park

The palms
are psalms.

The nail salons,
manicured lawns.

This is some phase.
The park has been razed.

I miss the hip,
hours at a clip,

their dopey glazed
Dolores haze

(sorry).
I worry

about basic stuff:
my graying scruff,

Ambien addiction.
Eviction . . .

—But there's another story:
this lawn was once a cemetery.

In 1888,
the late

were stirred,
disinterred,

carted somewhere calm, a
nothing place called Colma.

By then the dead
prohibited

in city light.
They thought this was all right:

the dead have nothing to lose;
the dead were Jews.

Hills of Eternity, Home of Peace:
the dead were put in their place.

Letters from Satilla

Diann Blakely, 1957–2014

1.

Have you read Andrew Hudgins' *After the Lost War*
or even Sidney Lanier's "The Marshes of Glynn"?
That's home for me. I'm married again,
but at times I think about buying one of those
Katrina Cottages and going alone to Birmingham,
my brother's backyard: my nieces and nephews
are my greatest joys, and I've never lived
in the same town as my real friends.
But we have a beautiful little farmhouse
literally picked up and moved here.
We're gated by an ungated community,
starter castles I only see when I leave
the house once a week for the doctors,
who inevitably mark the calendar.

2.

I have no left brain, and tend to think
like a cut-rate Henry James, progressing
associatively and constantly interrupting.
My mother is mad in precisely the same way.
Would she vote to legalize gay marriage?
Of course not. But in the early days
of AIDS, Mother was the primary organizer
of what I call the Casserole Brigade for Hairdressers.
She and her church group adored the men
who fixed them up each week at the Beauty Parlor.
She made sure her own hairdresser, who died,
as well as those of her friends',
were delivered casseroles daily, and did not remain
uncared-for during their illness. No indeed.

3.

If addiction is a form of suicide,
eight of my friends have committed suicide
over the past few years, starting with Deborah.
We didn't know each other well but bonded
over cigarettes (cigarettes!) at the Vermont winter
residency, held in Florida that year due to fears
of a lawsuit, after a writer slipped in Montpelier
and broke her hip. I have never heard
anyone scream quite as heart-stoppingly.
I was there in Florida to "substitute" (ridiculous
word, considering for whom) for Lynda Hull,
my great friend and mentor, after the wreck
crushed her feet and brought her back
to the needle that finally, indirectly, killed her.

4.

Ah well. Do keep those fashion notes coming.
I called Old Navy tonight and they were angels–
explained that I bought the spring line, and since
I'd dropped to 84 lbs., if they'd consider
taking it back, allowing me to buy "loungewear,"
I'd do everything in my power to secure them
a higher place in heaven. They couldn't have been nicer.
I'm sure you're busy–what do you do for a living
again?–but I miss you, dear friend. Have you ever
wanted to return to Gainesville for vacation?
I'm only four hours away. I can't leave my home,
but I love having visitors, and if you come
for a spell, I'll do my best to be well dressed–
I like to call it "invalid chic"–for the occasion.

Day into Night

Oh, this old thing? The heels are come hither,
But with balance. Still, the pencil skirt,
I know, makes my ass look like Yoko's,
That cover of *Double Fantasy*: flapjacks.
Uncle Bill did like the diversity of syrup
At IHOP. Somehow we always ended up there,
Rearranging the waxy dahlias.
You, with your nose in the packet:

Now's not the time for grief: he *was*
Old, in pop years. (Instead, think of that one
Twitchy day into night we ruled the baths.)
Irenic to the end, he held up one of his last
Cocktails (awful stuff) and said, rather like
Edmund White, "To all my tricks."

Renewal

Like patent protection;
like an erection.

Or the temp-controlled dead,
my mortician said.

The famine in our eyes;
the spawn of franchise.

EPITHALAMIUM

Remember the shake-the-salad days of *Dragnet*
reruns, spray and starch, and that pint-sized fridge?
Tenderloin Heights? The Earth Muffin magnet?
You stalked me on the Carquinez Bridge,

little Pinto; I asked you in to look at my iguana.
You stayed. You smelled like an arcade.
When I threatened to leave you for Guyana,
you swam all up in my Kool-Aid.

Even our losses felt relatively glam:
crullers, snap-on ties. Shadow gloves.
Your killer black Zodiac glasses.
A lot of meat, but not a lot of money, like Spam.
And our vinyl wedding, where doves
shot "A Blessing in Disguise" out of their rented asses.

SUMMER

Weeki Wachee, City of Live Mermaids

The job I chose:
a breathing hose;

a Lycra tail;
a sliding scale.

My lungs were bruised,
the light, diffused–

my somersault
was not at fault.

Before they let
me leave the set,

I took the plunge
to clean the *scrunge*,

our code for mold.
The waters hold

a clear and cold
account: untold,

the night, the pleas
of manatees

inscrutable. Dark
undid the park.

ALPHABET STREET

Prince Rogers Nelson, 1958–2016

"Adore" was my song
Back in '87–
Cool beans, I liked to say,
Desperately uncool.
Except for you.
Florida, a dirty hand
Gesture; the state, pay dirt.
Headphones on, I heard,
In a word, you were sex,
Just in time. Who was I
Kidding? Then, as now,
Love is too weak to define.
Mostly I just ran,
Not yet sixteen,
Overreaching. Track star,
Pretty uniform.
Queer, of course. *Adore.*
Rewind: my beloved teammates
Sometimes called me Cinnamon
Toast Crunch, or CTC, being neither black nor white.
Until the end of time.
Vanity would never do it for me.
Would you? You were definite, the
X in my fix. And now,
You're gone. The old, on repeat. The new
Zeal: zero.

TRANSLATION

So much has gone to shit. My hair. The state.
The addicts lie on Ellis Street, unfathered.
Reporters scribble synonyms for hate:
the men in blue have billy-clubbed the gathered.

And then, as grisly as an accident,
comes love, what feels like love. Befalls
the best of us, as if the discontent
of days were not enough. I make the calls,

or so I think: desire, that heretic,
is stealing, spider-fingered, all the hours.
The years. My scorn, acutely politic:
I peck him on the cheek, then hit the showers.

–Soapy, erect, I'll conjure up a time
when love was just a fecal, furtive crime.

Politics

My felon circumvents
　　the Nautilus machines–
mindless of the stylish,
　　wasting muscle queens–

and leans against the rack.
　　We study him like scholars.
As he removes his sweats,
　　I offer wadded dollars,

a petty cash advance.
　　All day he must equate
prosperity with flesh.
　　There's limited debate.

Young Republican

September, 1984.
The heat was like a ray-gun.
The Communists had much to fear:
his name was Ronald Reagan–

and so was mine in middle school,
throughout the mock debate.
The recreation hall was full
of democratic hate.

I ended all my thoughts with *well*,
declared my love for Nancy.
My stifling suit was poly-wool.
I sounded like a pansy.

But teachers didn't seem to care
that Ronald Reagan looked
a little fey, and had some flair.
I wanted to be liked,

the boy who mowed the neighbors' yards,
the new kid in Ocala–
while Mondale read his index cards,
I sipped a Coca Cola

that I had spiked with Mother's gin,
and frowned, and shook my head.
Oh Walter, there you go again,
I smiled and vainly said.

I reenacted getting shot.
I threw benign grenades.
I covered up what I forgot.
I never mentioned AIDS.

FISCAL

I hear it, the neighbor's kid discovering
notes on her recorder–repetitive, tortured,
like the onset of disappointment.

Or Art. Hear the 24, its groan up the hill.
This is Castro & Hill. The governor
five governors ago is governor again;

our shiny former mayor, his lieutenant.
Now comes the old man on a Segway,
his bag of groceries, sensible white helmet:

he's the closest thing I have to an angel.
He doesn't break a sweat, though it's hot–
September, Indian Summer, if it's all right

to call it that. It's not. The day
laborers have taken a break;
one eats a sack-lunch packed

nightly by his wife
in her outer-Mission life. Poetry
has the luxury of mythology.

This fiscal downturn is like Orpheus.
The twisted little boy-fucker. Like Orpheus,
I hear it, a voice receding, calling out,

the sound weak, infected–you choose,
doomed to the shades
of a preempted world. Turn around.

There is a sickness that is us.

Almost

One last meal, family style–
    no family, and with suspect style.
November first, my almost-groom
    fresh off his flasher costume
discharge at the office. Harris Tweed.
    I read it on his antisocial feed.

The motel life is all a dream–
    we were, as they say, living the dream.
I appreciate our quandary,
    hot-plate dates and frowsy laundry.
Face tattoos are never a good sign.
    I hope his tumor is benign.

I won't forget the time he lent
    me *Inches*, which I gave up for Lent.
Our love was threat, like phantom pain.
    An almost-plan for a bullet train.
I'm weaning myself off graphic tees,
    not taking on any new disease.

I walk along Pier 5 to kill the myth,
    of course another stab at myth.
I pull my output from the shelf
    and wildly anthologize myself.
I've adopted another yellow lab.
    I hope to die inside this cab.

My lack of faith is punctuation—
    no wait, the lack of punctuation.
Every intonation, one more pact
    with injury; my latest one-act:
Flossing in Public.
    In the spattered glass of the republic.

I Resign

I don't want any thing
or person, familiar or strange.
 −John Berryman

Like a lifeboat of easy marks,
like the ions and terror

of unmoving weather,
the moon on the water

a reputation
glaringly deficient,

I resign. I see: the difference
between doubt and democracy

is the time it takes to fan
cabbage for a spy-cam

at the bank. I walked in
like Helen Mirren

(dir. Peter Greenaway)−
smutty, grand, wounded−

sub-Helen-Mirren
in knockoff Gaultier.

I've chewed scenery in my day,
a sautoir nestled between

two bolt-on acquisitions.
I was brassy as a day job, hot

as yesterday's news...
All the reports are of drought

and hate-fucks. Fact is,
one day you're watching

the submarine races, the next,
duct-taped in the boiler room

of love, all uniform
role-play. So much

ordinary suffering.
Thirty years ago we were twacked

when we danced
to "Feed the world"–

we didn't feed ourselves,
much less the world.

But we had fun. There's a chance
we can have fun again.

Auto-tune is backing us up–
hand me your cup.

I've paid my taxes;
I've sent my faxes.

I gained a little access.
My version of subversion

is using two
exclamations when none will do;

that time I crimped my hair.
And then the cramped formality,

like a tell. There are moments of
grief standing in for grief.

I arrive only when I leave.
My street is a parklet,

my gym a hospice,
my deregulation

hub-and-spoke,
my shell a corporation.

Like a zombie gone
on a violent meditation retreat,

I resign. And if it rains,
when it does, it's not because:

it's savage as polite applause.

NOTES

"Nothing": The quoted line is from Miłosz's "Should, Should Not."

"Realtor": "House in Vermont" and "high-five" are slang for HIV.

"Halston": A few details are taken from *Simply Halston* by Steven Gaines.

"Fashion": The phrase "sex is mathematics" is from Bret Easton Ellis's *American Psycho*.

"Gainesville": The quoted lines are taken from Michael Hofmann's poem "Freebird."

"Day into Night": The quote from Edmund White is his dedication in *The Joy of Gay Sex*.

"Alphabet Street": This poem is for Sabina Piersol and Miguel Murphy.

"I Resign": The epigraph is taken from John Berryman's poem "He Resigns." The phrase "watching the submarine races" is a euphemism for making out in a parked car.